# Introduction 7

VBA for Word 365 for practitioners. Detailed instructions how to step-by-step customize examples.

VBA for Word 365 for practitioners. Detailed instructions how to step-by-step customize examples.

VBA for Word 365 for practitioners. Detailed instructions how to step-by-step customize examples.

VBA for Word 365 for practitioners. Detailed instructions how to step-by-step customize examples.

VBA for Word 365 for practitioners. Detailed instructions how to step-by-step customize examples.

VBA for Word 365 for practitioners. Detailed instructions how to step-by-step customize examples.

# Introduction

Depending on your specific needs, you can use VBA to automate a wide range of tasks, from simple text replacements to complex document formatting and data processing. It's a skill that can greatly enhance your productivity with Word.

I believe that practice is the best way to gain knowledge. Programming is a practical skill. You will get to know them faster and deeper when you read this book not in the light of a bedside lamp, but at the computer monitor. Step by step, without even realizing it, you will start working on more and more complex problems. Enjoy your time, have a fun with learning VBA.

# Hello, World!

VBA (Visual Basic for Applications) is a powerful tool for automating tasks in Microsoft Word. At the beginning some steps to help you get started:

**Step 1: Enable the Developer Tab**

1. Open Microsoft Word.

2. Go to the *File* tab.

3. Click on *Options*.

4. In the *Word Options* window, select *Customize Ribbon* on the left.

5. Check the box next to *Developer* in the right column.

6. Click *OK* to enable the Developer tab.

**Step 2: Open the Visual Basic for Applications Editor**

1. Click on the *Developer* tab in the ribbon.

2. Click on the *Visual Basic* button to open the VBA editor.

**Step 3: Create a New Module**

1. In the VBA editor, go to *Insert > Module* to create a new module.

**Step 4: Write Your First VBA Code**

The example will be classic. Paste this code into the module you created in Step 3.

VBA for Word 365 for practitioners. Detailed instructions how to step-by-step customize examples.

It displays a message box when you run it:

```
Sub HelloWorld()
    MsgBox "Hello, World!"
End Sub
```

### Step 5: Run Your VBA Code

1. Close the VBA editor.

2. Go back to your Word document.

3. Press *Alt + F8* to open the *Macro* dialog box.

4. Select *HelloWorld* (in this example or whatever you named your macro) from the list.

5. Click *Run* to execute the code.

You should see a message box that says *Hello, World!*

### Step 6: Edit and Debug Your Code

You can go back to the VBA editor to make changes and test your code further. The VBA editor provides tools for debugging, setting breakpoints, and watching variables.

### Step 7: Save Your Document with Macros

If you want to save your document with the VBA code, you should save it as a *Word Macro-Enabled Document* (.docm) to retain the code.

### Step 8: Learn and Explore

VBA is a powerful language, and there are many resources available online to learn more. Here are a few tips:

- Microsoft's official VBA documentation is a valuable resource.

- Websites and forums like Stack Overflow often have solutions to common VBA problems.

- Experiment with recording macros to see how Word generates VBA code for actions you perform manually.

This is just a basic introduction to VBA in Word. Repeat steps 1 through 7 every time you write code.

VBA for Word 365 for practitioners. Detailed instructions how to step-by-step customize examples.

# Options and variations

Here are some options and variations you can consider for the VBA code.

## Customize the message box title

You can specify a title for the message box using the *Title* argument of the *MsgBox* function:

```
Sub HelloWorldWithTitle()
    MsgBox "Hello, World!", vbInformation, "Greeting"
End Sub
```

In this example, the title of the message box will be *Greeting*.

## Use different message box buttons

You can specify different buttons for the message box using the Buttons argument:

```
Sub HelloWorldWithButtons()
    MsgBox "Hello, World!", vbYesNo + vbQuestion, "Question"
End Sub
```

In this example, the message box will have *Yes* and *No* buttons and will display a question icon.

## Customize the Icon

You can change the icon displayed in the message box using the *Icon* argument:

```
Sub HelloWorldWithIcon()
    MsgBox "Hello, World!", vbCritical, "Error"
End Sub
```

In this example, the message box will display a critical error icon.

## Store the message in a variable

You can store the message in a variable and then display it using the *MsgBox* function:

```
Sub HelloWorldWithVariable()
```

VBA for Word 365 for practitioners. Detailed instructions how to step-by-step customize examples.

```
    Dim greeting As String
    greeting = "Hello, World!"
    MsgBox greeting
End Sub
```

Variable has name *greeting*. Type of variable is *String*. This can be useful when you need to construct more complex messages dynamically.

## Add conditional logic

You can add conditional logic to your message window. For example, you can display different messages depending on the condition:

```
Sub GreetBasedOnTime()
    Dim currentTime As Date
    currentTime = Now

    If Hour(currentTime) < 12 Then
        MsgBox "Good morning!"
    Else
        MsgBox "Good afternoon!"
    End If
End Sub
```

This code greets the user differently depending on the current time.

## Close the document after displaying the message

You can add code to close the Word document automatically after displaying the message:

```
Sub HelloWorldAndCloseDocument()
    MsgBox "Hello, World!"
    ThisDocument.Close
End Sub
```

This code will close the currently open document after displaying the message.

## Input boxes

You can use input boxes to prompt the user for input. Here's an example that asks the user for their name and displays a customized greeting:

VBA for Word 365 for practitioners. Detailed instructions how to step-by-step customize examples.

```
Sub GreetUserWithInput()
    Dim userName As String
    userName = InputBox("Please enter your name:")

    If userName <> "" Then
        MsgBox "Hello, " & userName & "!"
    Else
        MsgBox "Hello, World!"
    End If
End Sub
```

This code uses the *InputBox* function to get user input.

## Looping

You can use loops in VBA to repeat actions. For example, the following code creates a numbered list of greetings:

```
Sub NumberedGreetings()
    Dim i As Integer
    Dim greeting As String

    For i = 1 To 5
        greeting = "Hello, World! " & i
        MsgBox greeting
    Next i
End Sub
```

This code uses a *For* loop to display the greeting multiple times. There is 5 repetitions in this example.

## Working with selection

You can interact with the selected text or the cursor position in a Word document. Here's an example that displays a message box with the selected text:

```
Sub ShowSelectedText()
    Dim selectedText As String
    selectedText = Selection.Text
```

VBA for Word 365 for practitioners. Detailed instructions how to step-by-step customize examples.

```vba
    If selectedText <> "" Then
        MsgBox "Selected Text: " & selectedText
    Else
        MsgBox "No text selected."
    End If
End Sub
```

This code retrieves and displays the selected text in a message box.

## Error handling

You can implement error handling to gracefully handle unexpected errors in your code. Here's a simple example:

```vba
Sub HandleError()
    On Error Resume Next
    Dim result As Integer
    result = 10 / 0 ' This will cause a runtime error

    If Err.Number <> 0 Then
        MsgBox "An error occurred: " & Err.Description,
vbExclamation, "Error"
        Err.Clear
    Else
        MsgBox "No error occurred."
    End If
    On Error GoTo 0
End Sub
```

This code uses *On Error Resume Next* to continue execution even if an error occurs, and then it checks for and handles the error.

These are just a few options and variations you can explore when working with VBA in Word. Depending on your specific needs, you can customize your VBA code to perform various tasks and interact with the user in different ways.

VBA for Word 365 for practitioners. Detailed instructions how to step-by-step customize examples.

# Working with document content

Let's take the next step in learning VBA in Word with some program examples. In this step, we'll focus on working with document content and manipulating text.

## Inserting text

You can use VBA to insert text into the active document. Here's an example that inserts a paragraph of text at the end of the document:

```
Sub InsertTextAtEnd()
    Selection.EndKey Unit:=wdStory
    Selection.TypeText Text:="This is a new paragraph inserted at
the end."
End Sub
```

## Options and variations

Here are some options and variations you can consider for the VBA code.

### Insert a different text

You can insert different text at the end of the document by changing the *Text* property:

```
Sub InsertDifferentTextAtEnd()
    Selection.EndKey Unit:=wdStory
    Selection.TypeText Text:="This is some different text inserted
at the end."
End Sub
```

This code inserts a different message at the end of the document.

### Insert multiple paragraphs

You can insert multiple paragraphs or lines of text at the end of the document:

```
Sub InsertMultipleParagraphsAtEnd()
    Selection.EndKey Unit:=wdStory
    Selection.TypeText Text:="Paragraph 1 inserted at the end."
```

VBA for Word 365 for practitioners. Detailed instructions how to step-by-step customize examples.

```
    Selection.TypeParagraph
    Selection.TypeText Text:="Paragraph 2 inserted at the end."
    Selection.TypeParagraph
    Selection.TypeText Text:="Paragraph 3 inserted at the end."
End Sub
```

This code inserts three paragraphs at the end of the document.

## Insert special characters

You can insert special characters or symbols at the end of the document:

```
Sub InsertSpecialCharactersAtEnd()
    Selection.EndKey Unit:=wdStory
    Selection.TypeText Text:="© 2022 My Company. All rights
reserved."
End Sub
```

This code inserts a copyright symbol and a copyright notice at the end of the document.

## Insert date and time

You can insert the current date and time at the end of the document:

```
Sub InsertDateAndTimeAtEnd()
    Selection.EndKey Unit:=wdStory
    Selection.TypeText Text:=Format(Now, "Long Date") & " " &
Format(Now, "Long Time")
End Sub
```

This code inserts the current date and time in a specific format at the end of the document.

## Insert content from another document

You can insert content from another document at the end of the current document. How it works? First code opens the source document and then use the Copy` and `Paste` methods:

```
Sub InsertContentFromAnotherDocument()
    Dim sourceDoc As Document
```

VBA for Word 365 for practitioners. Detailed instructions how to step-by-step customize examples.

```
    Set sourceDoc =
Documents.Open("C:\Path\To\Your\SourceDocument.docx")

    sourceDoc.Content.Copy
    Selection.EndKey Unit:=wdStory
    Selection.Paste
    sourceDoc.Close
End Sub
```

This code opens another document, copies it's content, and pastes it at the end of the current document.

## Insert text with hyperlinks

You can insert text with hyperlinks:

```
Sub InsertHyperlinkedTextAtEnd()
    Selection.EndKey Unit:=wdStory
    Selection.Hyperlinks.Add Anchor:=Selection.Range,
Address:="https://www.Amazon.com", TextToDisplay:="Visit
Amazon.com"
End Sub
```

This code inserts text with a hyperlink to a website at the end of the document.

## Insert formatted text using a style

You can insert formatted text using a predefined style:

```
Sub InsertStyledTextAtEnd()
    Selection.EndKey Unit:=wdStory
    Selection.Style = "Heading 1"
    Selection.TypeText Text:="This is styled text inserted at the
end using the 'Heading 1' style."
End Sub
```

This code inserts text with the *Heading 1* style applied.

## Insert text as a table

You can insert text as a table at the end of the document:

VBA for Word 365 for practitioners. Detailed instructions how to step-by-step customize examples.

```vba
Sub InsertTextAsTableAtEnd()
    Selection.EndKey Unit:=wdStory
    Selection.TypeText Text:="Creating a table at the end of the
document:"
    Selection.TypeParagraph
    Selection.Tables.Add Range:=Selection.Range, NumRows:=3,
NumColumns:=3
End Sub
```

This code inserts a message and then creates a 3x3 table at the end of the document.

## Finding and replacing text

VBA can automate the process of finding and replacing text. Here's an example that finds and replaces text in the document:

```vba
Sub FindAndReplace()
    With Selection.Find
        .Text = "oldText"
        .Replacement.Text = "newText"
        .Forward = True
        .Wrap = wdFindContinue
        .Execute Replace:=wdReplaceAll
    End With
End Sub
```

## Advanced find and replace

VBA allows you to perform advanced find and replace operations using regular expressions. Here's an example that finds and highlights all email addresses in a document:

```vba
Sub FindAndHighlightEmails()
    With Selection.Find
        .ClearFormatting
        .Text = "[A-Za-z0-9._%+-]+@[A-Za-z0-9.-]+\.[A-Za-z]{2,4}"
        .Replacement.ClearFormatting
        .Replacement.Highlight = True
```

VBA for Word 365 for practitioners. Detailed instructions how to step-by-step customize examples.

```
        .Forward = True
        .Wrap = wdFindStop
        .Format = True
        .MatchWildcards = True
        .Execute Replace:=wdReplaceAll
    End With
End Sub
```

# Formatting text

## Insert text with specific formatting

You can insert text with specific formatting, such as font size, color, and style:

```
Sub InsertFormattedTextAtEnd()
    Selection.EndKey Unit:=wdStory
    Selection.Font.Size = 14
    Selection.Font.Color = RGB(255, 0, 0) ' Red
    Selection.Font.Bold = True
    Selection.TypeText Text:="This is formatted text inserted at
the end."
End Sub
```

This code inserts text with a larger font size, red color, and bold style at the end of the document.

## Options and variations

Here are some options and variations you can consider for the VBA code.

### Insert text in a specific font style

You can insert text using a specific font style:

```
Sub InsertTextWithFontStyleAtEnd()
    Selection.EndKey Unit:=wdStory
    Selection.Font.Name = "Arial"
    Selection.TypeText Text:="This is text in the Arial font
inserted at the end."
```

```
End Sub
```

This code inserts text using the *Arial* font style at the end of the document.

## Toggle bold formatting

You can modify the code to toggle the bold formatting of the selected text. If the text is already bold, it will remove the bold formatting, and if it's not bold, it will make it bold:

```
Sub ToggleBold()
    If Selection.Type = wdSelectionText Then
        Selection.Font.Bold = Not Selection.Font.Bold
    End If
End Sub
```

This code toggles the bold formatting of the selected text.

## Apply bold to specific keywords

You can apply bold formatting only to specific keywords or phrases within the selected text:

```
Sub ApplyBoldToKeywords()
    If Selection.Type = wdSelectionText Then
        Dim keywords() As String
        keywords = Split("important,urgent", ",")

        Dim word As Variant
        For Each word In keywords
            Selection.Find.ClearFormatting
            With Selection.Find
                .Text = word
                .Replacement.Font.Bold = True
                .Replacement.Text = "^&"
                .Forward = True
                .Wrap = wdFindStop
                .Format = True
            End With
            Selection.Find.Execute Replace:=wdReplaceAll
```

VBA for Word 365 for practitioners. Detailed instructions how to step-by-step customize examples.

```
        Next word
    End If
End Sub
```

This code searches for specific keywords (e.g., "important" or "urgent") within the selected text and makes them bold.

## Apply Other Formatting

You can extend the code to apply other formatting changes along with bold, such as changing the font color or size:

```
Sub ApplyFormatting()
    If Selection.Type = wdSelectionText Then
        With Selection.Font
            .Bold = True
            .Color = RGB(255, 0, 0) ' Red
            .Size = 14
        End With
    End If
End Sub
```

This code makes the selected text bold, changes the text color to red, and increases the font size to 14.

## Apply Different Styles

You can apply different predefined styles to the selected text:

```
Sub ApplyDifferentStyles()
    If Selection.Type = wdSelectionText Then
        Selection.Style = "Strong" ' Apply the "Strong" style
    End If
End Sub
```

This code applies the *Strong* style to the selected text, which is a predefined style in Word.

VBA for Word 365 for practitioners. Detailed instructions how to step-by-step customize examples.

## Apply conditional formatting

You can apply formatting conditionally based on certain criteria. For example, you can make text bold only if it contains a specific keyword:

```
Sub ConditionalFormatting()
    If Selection.Type = wdSelectionText Then
        If InStr(1, Selection.Text, "important", vbTextCompare) >
0 Then
            Selection.Bold = True
        End If
    End If
End Sub
```

This code makes the selected text bold only if it contains the word *important*.

## Apply formatting to entire paragraph

You can apply formatting not only to the selected text but to the entire paragraph containing the selection:

```
Sub FormatParagraph()
    If Selection.Type = wdSelectionText Then
        Selection.Paragraphs(1).Range.Bold = True
    End If
End Sub
```

This code makes the entire paragraph containing the selected text bold.

## Apply formatting to multiple selections

You can modify the code to apply bold formatting to multiple selected text ranges:

```
Sub ApplyBoldToMultipleSelections()
    Dim selectedRange As Range
    For Each selectedRange In Selection.Range
        If selectedRange.Type = wdSelectionText Then
            selectedRange.Font.Bold = True
```

```
        End If
    Next selectedRange
End Sub
```

This code iterates through all selected text ranges and makes each of them bold.

## Toggle bold for entire paragraphs

Instead of applying bold to selected text within a paragraph, you can toggle the bold formatting for entire paragraphs:

```
Sub ToggleBoldForParagraphs()
    Dim paragraph As Paragraph
    For Each paragraph In Selection.Paragraphs
        paragraph.Range.Font.Bold = Not paragraph.Range.Font.Bold
    Next paragraph
End Sub
```

This code toggles the bold formatting for entire paragraphs within the selection.

## Apply bold to headings

You can target specific styles, such as headings, to apply bold formatting:

```
Sub ApplyBoldToHeadings()
    Dim paragraph As Paragraph
    For Each paragraph In Selection.Paragraphs
        If paragraph.Style = "Heading 1" Or paragraph.Style =
"Heading 2" Then
            paragraph.Range.Font.Bold = True
        End If
    Next paragraph
End Sub
```

This code makes headings (styles *Heading 1* and *Heading 2*) within the selection bold.

## Remove bold formatting

You can create a code to remove bold formatting from selected text:

VBA for Word 365 for practitioners. Detailed instructions how to step-by-step customize examples.

```
Sub RemoveBoldFormatting()
    If Selection.Type = wdSelectionText Then
        Selection.Font.Bold = False
    End If
End Sub
```

This code removes bold formatting from the selected text if it's currently bold.

These options allow you to customize the code to apply various formatting changes to the selected text or paragraphs based on your specific requirements. You can combine different formatting properties and conditions as needed.

# Working with tables

If your document contains tables, you can use VBA to manipulate table data. Here's an example that adds a new row to a table:

```
Sub AddRowToTable()
    Dim tbl As Table
    Set tbl = ActiveDocument.Tables(1) ' Change the index to the
table you want to work with

    tbl.Rows.Add
    ' You can further manipulate the new row here
End Sub
```

## Options and variations

Here are some examples of tasks you can perform when working with tables in Word using VBA.

### Create a new table

```
Sub CreateNewTable()
    Dim tbl As Table
    Set tbl = ActiveDocument.Tables.Add(Selection.Range,
NumRows:=3, NumColumns:=4)
    ' Customize table properties (e.g., borders, cell spacing,
etc.) here if needed
```

VBA for Word 365 for practitioners. Detailed instructions how to step-by-step customize examples.

```
End Sub
```

This code creates a new table with 3 rows and 4 columns at the current selection point.

## Insert data into a table

```
Sub InsertDataIntoTable()
    Dim tbl As Table
    Set tbl = ActiveDocument.Tables(1) ' Assumes the table is the
first table in the document
    tbl.Cell(1, 1).Range.Text = "Header 1"
    tbl.Cell(1, 2).Range.Text = "Header 2"
    tbl.Cell(1, 3).Range.Text = "Header 3"
    ' Add more data to the table here
End Sub
```

This code inserts data into specific cells of an existing table.

## Format table cells

```
Sub FormatTableCells()
    Dim tbl As Table
    Set tbl = ActiveDocument.Tables(1)

    ' Apply formatting to the entire table or specific cells
    tbl.Borders.Enable = True
    tbl.Rows(1).Shading.BackgroundPatternColor = RGB(200, 200,
200)
    tbl.Cell(2, 2).Range.Font.Bold = True
    ' Apply more formatting as needed
End Sub
```

This code demonstrates how to format table cells by enabling borders, shading rows, and making specific cells bold.

## Delete a table

```
Sub DeleteTable()
    Dim tbl As Table
```

VBA for Word 365 for practitioners. Detailed instructions how to step-by-step customize examples.

```
Set tbl = ActiveDocument.Tables(1)
tbl.Delete
End Sub
```

This code deletes the first table in the document. You can modify it to delete a specific table by changing the index.

## Loop through table data

```
Sub LoopThroughTableData()
    Dim tbl As Table
    Dim row As Row, cell As Cell
    Set tbl = ActiveDocument.Tables(1)

    For Each row In tbl.Rows
        For Each cell In row.Cells
            Debug.Print cell.Range.Text
        Next cell
    Next row
End Sub
```

This code loops through all the cells in the first table of the document and prints the text in each cell to the Immediate window.

## Sort table data

```
Sub SortTableData()
    Dim tbl As Table
    Set tbl = ActiveDocument.Tables(1)

    tbl.Sort SortOrder:=wdSortOrderAscending, FieldNumber:=1
End Sub
```

This code sorts the data in the first table of the document in ascending order based on the first column.

## Autofit table to content

```
Sub AutofitTableToContent()
    Dim tbl As Table
```

VBA for Word 365 for practitioners. Detailed instructions how to step-by-step customize examples.

```
    Set tbl = ActiveDocument.Tables(1)


    ' Autofit the table to its content
    tbl.AutoFitBehavior (wdAutoFitContent)
End Sub
```

This code automatically adjusts the width of the cells in the first table of the document to fit the content.

## Merge and split cells

```
Sub MergeAndSplitCells()
    Dim tbl As Table
    Set tbl = ActiveDocument.Tables(1)


    ' Merge cells in the first row
    tbl.Cell(1, 1).Merge MergeTo:=tbl.Cell(1, 2)


    ' Split a merged cell
    tbl.Cell(1, 1).Split NumRows:=2, NumColumns:=2
End Sub
```

This code demonstrates how to merge and split cells within a table.

## Insert row and column

```
Sub InsertRowAndColumn()
    Dim tbl As Table
    Set tbl = ActiveDocument.Tables(1)


    ' Insert a new row after the second row
    tbl.Rows(2).Select
    Selection.InsertRowsBelow


    ' Insert a new column after the third column
    tbl.Columns(3).Select
    Selection.InsertColumnsRight
End Sub
```

VBA for Word 365 for practitioners. Detailed instructions how to step-by-step customize examples.

This code inserts a new row below the second row and a new column to the right of the third column in the table.

## Copy data between tables

```
Sub CopyDataBetweenTables()
    Dim sourceTbl As Table
    Dim targetTbl As Table
    Set sourceTbl = ActiveDocument.Tables(1)
    Set targetTbl = ActiveDocument.Tables(2)

    ' Copy data from the first cell of the source table to the
second cell of the target table
    sourceTbl.Cell(1, 1).Range.Copy
    targetTbl.Cell(1, 2).Range.Paste
End Sub
```

This code copies data from one cell in the source table to another cell in the target table.

## Format specific rows based on criteria

```
Sub FormatRowsBasedOnCriteria()
    Dim tbl As Table
    Set tbl = ActiveDocument.Tables(1)

    Dim row As Row

    ' Format rows where the value in the second column is greater
than 50
    For Each row In tbl.Rows
        If CDbl(row.Cells(2).Range.Text) > 50 Then
            row.Shading.BackgroundPatternColor = RGB(255, 0, 0) '
Red background
            row.Cells(2).Range.Font.Bold = True ' Bold text in the
second column
        End If
    Next row
```

```
End Sub
```

This code formats rows in a table where the value in the second column meets a specific criteria (e.g., greater than 50).

These examples should give you a good starting point for working with tables in Word using VBA. You can adapt and combine these techniques to perform more complex table-related tasks as needed.

# Counting words

You can use VBA to count the number of words in a document:

```
Sub CountWords()
    Dim wordCount As Integer
    wordCount = ActiveDocument.Words.Count

    MsgBox "Total word count: " & wordCount
End Sub
```

## Options and variations

Here are some examples of tasks you can perform when counting words in Word using VBA.

### Count words in a selection

```
Sub CountWordsInSelection()
    Dim wordCount As Integer
    wordCount = Selection.Words.Count

    MsgBox "Word count in selection: " & wordCount
End Sub
```

This code counts the words within the currently selected text in the document.

### Count words in a specific paragraph

```
Sub CountWordsInParagraph()
    Dim wordCount As Integer
    Dim para As Paragraph
```

VBA for Word 365 for practitioners. Detailed instructions how to step-by-step customize examples.

```
    ' Assuming you want to count words in the second paragraph
    Set para = ActiveDocument.Paragraphs(2)

    wordCount = para.Range.Words.Count

    MsgBox "Word count in paragraph: " & wordCount
End Sub
```

This code counts the words within a specific paragraph in the document.

## Count words in a table cell

```
Sub CountWordsInTableCell()
    Dim wordCount As Integer
    Dim tbl As Table
    Dim cell As Cell

    ' Assuming you want to count words in the second cell of the
first table
    Set tbl = ActiveDocument.Tables(1)
    Set cell = tbl.Cell(1, 2)

    wordCount = cell.Range.Words.Count

    MsgBox "Word count in table cell: " & wordCount
End Sub
```

This code counts the words within a specific table cell in the document.

## Count words in a specific heading style

```
Sub CountWordsInHeadingStyle()
    Dim wordCount As Integer
    Dim rng As Range

    ' Define the range based on a specific heading style (e.g.,
"Heading 1")
```

VBA for Word 365 for practitioners. Detailed instructions how to step-by-step customize examples.

```
    Set rng = ActiveDocument.Styles("Heading
1").Paragraphs(1).Range

    wordCount = rng.Words.Count

    MsgBox "Word count in 'Heading 1': " & wordCount
End Sub
```

This code counts the words within the first paragraph that uses the "Heading 1" style.

## Count words in a specific comment

```
Sub CountWordsInComment()
    Dim wordCount As Integer
    Dim comment As Comment

    ' Assuming you want to count words in the first comment in the
document
    Set comment = ActiveDocument.Comments(1)

    wordCount = comment.Scope.Words.Count

    MsgBox "Word count in comment: " & wordCount
End Sub
```

This code counts the words within the text of a specific comment in the document.

## Count words in footnotes or endnotes

```
Sub CountWordsInFootnotesOrEndnotes()
    Dim wordCount As Integer
    Dim note As Footnote

    ' Assuming you want to count words in the first footnote
    Set note = ActiveDocument.Footnotes(1)

    wordCount = note.Range.Words.Count
```

```
    MsgBox "Word count in footnote: " & wordCount
End Sub
```

This code counts the words within the text of a specific footnote in the document.

## Count words in text boxes

```
Sub CountWordsInTextBox()
    Dim wordCount As Integer
    Dim textBox As Shape

    ' Assuming you want to count words in the first text box in
the document
    Set textBox = ActiveDocument.Shapes(1)

    wordCount = textBox.TextFrame.TextRange.Words.Count

    MsgBox "Word count in text box: " & wordCount
End Sub
```

This code counts the words within the text of a specific text box in the document.

## Count words in headers or footers

```
Sub CountWordsInHeaderOrFooter()
    Dim wordCount As Integer
    Dim headerRange As Range

    ' Assuming you want to count words in the primary header of
the first section
    Set headerRange =
ActiveDocument.Sections(1).Headers(wdHeaderFooterPrimary).Range

    wordCount = headerRange.Words.Count

    MsgBox "Word count in header: " & wordCount
```

VBA for Word 365 for practitioners. Detailed instructions how to step-by-step customize examples.

```
End Sub
```

This code counts the words within the primary header of the first section in the document.

## Count words excluding headers and footers

```
Sub CountWordsExcludingHeadersFooters()
    Dim wordCount As Integer

    ' Calculate word count excluding headers and footers
    wordCount = ActiveDocument.Content.Words.Count

    MsgBox "Word count excluding headers and footers: " &
wordCount
End Sub
```

This code counts the words in the main document content, excluding text in headers and footers.

These options allow you to count words in various contexts within a Word document, including selections, paragraphs, custom ranges, document sections, and table cells. You can adapt the code to suit your specific word counting needs in different parts of the document.

# Working with variables

Variables are used to store and manipulate data in VBA. Here's an example that calculates the sum of two numbers:

```
Sub CalculateSum()
    Dim num1 As Double
    Dim num2 As Double
    Dim result As Double

    num1 = 10
    num2 = 20
    result = num1 + num2

    MsgBox "The sum is " & result
```

VBA for Word 365 for practitioners. Detailed instructions how to step-by-step customize examples.

```
End Sub
```

# Options and variations

Here are some options and variations you can consider for the VBA code.

## Calculate and display the difference

```
Sub CalculateDifference()
    Dim num1 As Double
    Dim num2 As Double
    Dim result As Double

    num1 = 20
    num2 = 10
    result = num1 - num2

    MsgBox "The difference is " & result
End Sub
```

This code calculates the difference between *num1* and *num2* and displays it in a message box.

## Calculate and display the product

```
Sub CalculateProduct()
    Dim num1 As Double
    Dim num2 As Double
    Dim result As Double

    num1 = 10
    num2 = 20
    result = num1 * num2

    MsgBox "The product is " & result
End Sub
```

This code calculates the product of *num1* and *num2* and displays it in a message box.

VBA for Word 365 for practitioners. Detailed instructions how to step-by-step customize examples.

## Calculate and display the division

```
Sub CalculateDivision()
    Dim num1 As Double
    Dim num2 As Double
    Dim result As Double

    num1 = 20
    num2 = 10
    result = num1 / num2

    MsgBox "The division result is " & result
End Sub
```

This code calculates the result of dividing *num1* by *num2* and displays it in a message box.

## Calculate and display the average

```
Sub CalculateAverage()
    Dim num1 As Double
    Dim num2 As Double
    Dim result As Double

    num1 = 10
    num2 = 20
    result = (num1 + num2) / 2

    MsgBox "The average is " & result
End Sub
```

This code calculates the average of *num1* and *num2* and displays it in a message box.

## Calculate and display the square root

```
Sub CalculateSquareRoot()
    Dim num1 As Double
    Dim result As Double
```

```
    num1 = 25
    result = Sqr(num1)

    MsgBox "The square root is " & result
End Sub
```

This code calculates the square root of *num1* and displays it in a message box.

## Accept user input

```
Sub CalculateSumWithInput()
    Dim num1 As Double
    Dim num2 As Double
    Dim result As Double

    ' Prompt the user for input
    num1 = InputBox("Enter the first number:")
    num2 = InputBox("Enter the second number:")

    ' Check if user canceled input
    If num1 = "" Or num2 = "" Then
        MsgBox "Input canceled."
    Else
        ' Convert input to numbers and calculate the sum
        num1 = CDbl(num1)
        num2 = CDbl(num2)
        result = num1 + num2
        MsgBox "The sum is " & result
    End If
End Sub
```

This code prompts the user to enter two numbers and calculates their sum. It also checks if the user cancels the input.

## Calculate sum with user input

```
Sub CalculateSumWithInput()
    Dim num1 As Double
```

VBA for Word 365 for practitioners. Detailed instructions how to step-by-step customize examples.

```
    Dim num2 As Double
    Dim result As Double

    ' Prompt the user to enter two numbers
    num1 = InputBox("Enter the first number:")
    num2 = InputBox("Enter the second number:")

    ' Check if the user canceled the input or entered non-numeric
values
    If IsNumeric(num1) And IsNumeric(num2) Then
        result = CDbl(num1) + CDbl(num2)
        MsgBox "The sum is " & result
    Else
        MsgBox "Invalid input. Please enter numeric values."
    End If
End Sub
```

This code prompts the user to enter two numbers, performs the calculation, and displays the result in a message box. It also includes input validation.

## Calculate sum of numbers from a range

```
Sub CalculateSumFromRange()
    Dim rng As Range
    Dim result As Double

    ' Define a range of cells with numbers
    Set rng = ActiveDocument.Range(Start:=10, End:=30) ' Adjust
the range as needed

    ' Calculate the sum of numbers in the range
    result = WorksheetFunction.Sum(rng.Words)

    MsgBox "The sum of numbers in the range is " & result
End Sub
```

This code calculates the sum of numbers within a specified range of text in the document.

VBA for Word 365 for practitioners. Detailed instructions how to step-by-step customize examples.

## Calculate sum with decimal places

```
Sub CalculateSumWithDecimal()
    Dim num1 As Double
    Dim num2 As Double
    Dim result As Double

    num1 = 10.5
    num2 = 20.75
    result = num1 + num2

    MsgBox "The sum is " & Format(result, "0.00")
End Sub
```

This code calculates the sum of two numbers with decimal places and displays the result formatted to two decimal places.

## Calculate sum using a function

```
Function CalculateSumFunction(num1 As Double, num2 As Double) As Double
    CalculateSumFunction = num1 + num2
End Function


Sub CallCalculateSumFunction()
    Dim num1 As Double
    Dim num2 As Double
    Dim result As Double

    num1 = 10
    num2 = 20
    result = CalculateSumFunction(num1, num2)

    MsgBox "The sum is " & result
End Sub
```

This code defines a custom function to calculate the sum of two numbers and then calls that function in a separate subroutine.

VBA for Word 365 for practitioners. Detailed instructions how to step-by-step customize examples.

These options provide variations of the original code to perform different mathematical operations and handle user input. You can adapt the code to perform various calculations and display results as needed.

# Input validation

Input validation in VBA for Word can help ensure that the user enters valid data when prompted. Here's an example of how to perform input validation when asking the user for numeric input:

```
Sub ValidateNumericInput()
    Dim userInput As Variant
    Dim isValidInput As Boolean
    Dim result As Double

    ' Prompt the user for input
    Do
        userInput = InputBox("Enter a numeric value:")

        ' Check if the user canceled the input
        If userInput = "" Then
            MsgBox "Input canceled. Exiting."
            Exit Sub
        End If

        ' Attempt to convert the input to a numeric value
        On Error Resume Next
        result = CDbl(userInput)
        On Error GoTo 0

        ' Check if the conversion was successful
        If IsNumeric(result) Then
            isValidInput = True
        Else
            MsgBox "Invalid input. Please enter a numeric value."
            isValidInput = False
        End If
```

```
    Loop While Not isValidInput


    ' Process the valid numeric input
    MsgBox "You entered a valid numeric value: " & result
End Sub
```

In this example

1. The *InputBox* function is used to prompt the user for input.

2. The code checks if the user canceled the input by checking if the input is an empty string (`""`).

3. It attempts to convert the user's input to a numeric value using *CDbl*.

4. If the conversion is successful (i.e., *IsNumeric(result)* is *True* ), the input is considered valid, and the loop exits.

5. If the conversion fails, the code displays an error message, sets *isValidInput* to *False*, and continues to prompt the user until valid input is provided.

6. Once valid input is obtained, the code proceeds to process it.

You can modify this code to suit your specific input validation requirements or to validate input for different data types or formats.

# Options and variations

Here are some options and variations you can consider for the VBA code.

## Validate positive integer input

```
Sub ValidatePositiveIntegerInput()
    Dim userInput As Variant
    Dim isValidInput As Boolean
    Dim result As Integer


    ' Prompt the user for input
    Do
        userInput = InputBox("Enter a positive integer:")


        ' Check if the user canceled the input
```

```
        If userInput = "" Then
            MsgBox "Input canceled. Exiting."
            Exit Sub
        End If


        ' Attempt to convert the input to an integer
        On Error Resume Next
        result = CInt(userInput)
        On Error GoTo 0


        ' Check if the conversion was successful and the input is
positive
        If IsNumeric(result) And result > 0 Then
            isValidInput = True
        Else
            MsgBox "Invalid input. Please enter a positive
integer."
            isValidInput = False
        End If
    Loop While Not isValidInput


    ' Process the valid input
    MsgBox "You entered a valid positive integer: " & result
End Sub
```

This code specifically validates that the user enters a positive integer.

## Validate email address input

```
Sub ValidateEmailAddressInput()
    Dim userInput As Variant
    Dim isValidInput As Boolean
    Dim emailPattern As String
    Dim regex As Object


    ' Define the regular expression pattern for email validation
```

VBA for Word 365 for practitioners. Detailed instructions how to step-by-step customize examples.

```
    emailPattern = "^\w+([-+.']\w+)*@\w+([-.]\w+)*\.\w+([-
.]\w+)*$"


    ' Create a Regular Expression object
    Set regex = CreateObject("VBScript.RegExp")
    regex.Global = False
    regex.IgnoreCase = True
    regex.Pattern = emailPattern


    ' Prompt the user for input
    Do
        userInput = InputBox("Enter an email address:")


        ' Check if the user canceled the input
        If userInput = "" Then
            MsgBox "Input canceled. Exiting."
            Exit Sub
        End If


        ' Check if the input matches the email pattern
        If regex.Test(userInput) Then
            isValidInput = True
        Else
            MsgBox "Invalid input. Please enter a valid email
address."
            isValidInput = False
        End If
    Loop While Not isValidInput


    ' Process the valid email address input
    MsgBox "You entered a valid email address: " & userInput
End Sub
```

This code validates that the user enters a valid email address using a regular expression pattern.

VBA for Word 365 for practitioners. Detailed instructions how to step-by-step customize examples.

## Validate date input

```
Sub ValidateDateInput()
    Dim userInput As Variant
    Dim isValidInput As Boolean
    Dim result As Date

    ' Prompt the user for input
    Do
        userInput = InputBox("Enter a date (mm/dd/yyyy format):")

        ' Check if the user canceled the input
        If userInput = "" Then
            MsgBox "Input canceled. Exiting."
            Exit Sub
        End If

        ' Attempt to convert the input to a Date
        On Error Resume Next
        result = CDate(userInput)
        On Error GoTo 0

        ' Check if the conversion was successful
        If IsDate(result) Then
            isValidInput = True
        Else
            MsgBox "Invalid input. Please enter a valid date in
mm/dd/yyyy format."
            isValidInput = False
        End If
    Loop While Not isValidInput

    ' Process the valid date input
    MsgBox "You entered a valid date: " & Format(result,
"mm/dd/yyyy")
End Sub
```

VBA for Word 365 for practitioners. Detailed instructions how to step-by-step customize examples.

This code validates that the user enters a valid date in mm/dd/yyyy format.

## Validate alphanumeric input

```
Sub ValidateAlphanumericInput()
    Dim userInput As Variant
    Dim isValidInput As Boolean
    Dim alphanumericPattern As String
    Dim regex As Object

    ' Define the regular expression pattern for alphanumeric
validation
    alphanumericPattern = "^[A-Za-z0-9]+$"

    ' Create a Regular Expression object
    Set regex = CreateObject("VBScript.RegExp")
    regex.Global = False
    regex.IgnoreCase = True
    regex.Pattern = alphanumericPattern

    ' Prompt the user for input
    Do
        userInput = InputBox("Enter an alphanumeric value:")

        ' Check if the user canceled the input
        If userInput = "" Then
            MsgBox "Input canceled. Exiting."
            Exit Sub
        End If

        ' Check if the input matches the alphanumeric pattern
        If regex.Test(userInput) Then
            isValidInput = True
        Else
            MsgBox "Invalid input. Please enter a valid
alphanumeric value."
```

```
        isValidInput = False
    End If
Loop While Not isValidInput


' Process the valid alphanumeric input
MsgBox "You entered a valid alphanumeric value: " & userInput
End Sub
```

This code validates that the user enters a valid alphanumeric value using a regular expression pattern.

# Validate password strength

```
Sub ValidatePasswordStrength()
    Dim userInput As Variant
    Dim isValidInput As Boolean
    Dim passwordStrengthPattern As String
    Dim regex As Object


    ' Define the regular expression pattern for password strength
validation
    passwordStrengthPattern = "^(?=.*[A-Z])(?=.*[a-
z])(?=.*\d)(?=.*[@$!%*?&])[A-Za-z\d@$!%*?&]{8,}$"


    ' Create a Regular Expression object
    Set regex = CreateObject("VBScript.RegExp")
    regex.Global = False
    regex.IgnoreCase = True
    regex.Pattern = passwordStrengthPattern


    ' Prompt the user for input
    Do
        userInput = InputBox("Enter a password with at least 8
characters, including uppercase, lowercase, digits, and special
characters:")


        ' Check if the user canceled the input
```

VBA for Word 365 for practitioners. Detailed instructions how to step-by-step customize examples.

```vba
        If userInput = "" Then
            MsgBox "Input canceled. Exiting."
            Exit Sub
        End If


        ' Check if the input matches the password strength pattern
        If regex.Test(userInput) Then
            isValidInput = True
        Else
            MsgBox "Invalid input. Please enter a password that
meets the specified criteria."
            isValidInput = False
        End If
    Loop While Not isValidInput


    ' Process the valid password input
    MsgBox "You entered a valid password."
End Sub
```

This code validates the strength of a user-entered password based on specified criteria using a regular expression pattern.

These options demonstrate how to perform input validation for different types of data, such as positive integers and email addresses. You can adapt and customize the code to validate various types of user input based on your specific requirements.

## Validate file path input

```vba
Sub ValidateFilePathInput()
    Dim userInput As Variant
    Dim isValidInput As Boolean

    ' Prompt the user for input
    Do
        userInput = InputBox("Enter a file path:")

        ' Check if the user canceled the input
```

VBA for Word 365 for practitioners. Detailed instructions how to step-by-step customize examples.

```vba
        If userInput = "" Then
            MsgBox "Input canceled. Exiting."
            Exit Sub
        End If


        ' Check if the input represents a valid file path
        If Len(Dir(userInput)) > 0 Then
            isValidInput = True
        Else
            MsgBox "Invalid input. Please enter a valid file
path."
            isValidInput = False
        End If
    Loop While Not isValidInput


    ' Process the valid file path input
    MsgBox "You entered a valid file path: " & userInput
End Sub
```

This code validates that the user enters a valid file path by checking if the file exists.

## Validate Yes/No input

```vba
Sub ValidateYesNoInput()
    Dim userInput As Variant
    Dim isValidInput As Boolean


    ' Prompt the user for input
    Do
        userInput = UCase(InputBox("Enter 'Yes' or 'No':"))


        ' Check if the user canceled the input
        If userInput = "" Then
            MsgBox "Input canceled. Exiting."
            Exit Sub
        End If
```

```
        ' Check if the input is 'Yes' or 'No'
        If userInput = "YES" Or userInput = "NO" Then
            isValidInput = True
        Else
            MsgBox "Invalid input. Please enter 'Yes' or 'No'."
            isValidInput = False
        End If
    Loop While Not isValidInput

    ' Process the valid Yes/No input
    MsgBox "You entered: " & userInput
End Sub
```

This code validates that the user enters either *Yes* or *No* (case-insensitive).

# Validate input using a custom function

```
Function IsInputValid(input As String) As Boolean
    ' Add custom validation logic here
    ' For example, check if the input meets certain criteria
    ' Return True if valid, False if not
    IsInputValid = (Len(input) >= 5) And (Len(input) <= 10)
End Function

Sub ValidateCustomInput()
    Dim userInput As Variant
    Dim isValidInput As Boolean

    ' Prompt the user for input
    Do
        userInput = InputBox("Enter custom input (between 5 and 10
characters):")

        ' Check if the user canceled the input
        If userInput = "" Then
            MsgBox "Input canceled. Exiting."
```

VBA for Word 365 for practitioners. Detailed instructions how to step-by-step customize examples.

```
        Exit Sub
    End If


    ' Check if the input is valid using the custom function
    If IsInputValid(userInput) Then
        isValidInput = True
    Else
        MsgBox "Invalid input. Please enter input that meets
the specified criteria."
        isValidInput = False
    End If
    Loop While Not isValidInput


    ' Process the valid custom input
    MsgBox "You entered valid custom input: " & userInput
End Sub
```

In this option, a custom function *IsInputValid* is used to validate the user input based on custom criteria.

These additional options offer different types of input validation scenarios, including file paths, Yes/No responses, and custom validation using functions. You can customize these examples to suit your specific validation requirements.

## Validate phone number input

```
Sub ValidatePhoneNumberInput()
    Dim userInput As Variant
    Dim isValidInput As Boolean
    Dim phoneNumberPattern As String
    Dim regex As Object


    ' Define the regular expression pattern for phone number
validation (U.S. format)
    phoneNumberPattern = "^\d{3}-\d{3}-\d{4}$"


    ' Create a Regular Expression object
```

VBA for Word 365 for practitioners. Detailed instructions how to step-by-step customize examples.

```
Set regex = CreateObject("VBScript.RegExp")
regex.Global = False
regex.IgnoreCase = True
regex.Pattern = phoneNumberPattern


' Prompt the user for input
Do
    userInput = InputBox("Enter a phone number in the format
'xxx-xxx-xxxx' (U.S. format):")


    ' Check if the user canceled the input
    If userInput = "" Then
        MsgBox "Input canceled. Exiting."
        Exit Sub
    End If


    ' Check if the input matches the phone number pattern
    If regex.Test(userInput) Then
        isValidInput = True
    Else
        MsgBox "Invalid input. Please enter a valid phone
number in the format 'xxx-xxx-xxxx' (U.S. format)."
        isValidInput = False
    End If
Loop While Not isValidInput


' Process the valid phone number input
MsgBox "You entered a valid phone number: " & userInput
End Sub
```

This code validates that the user enters a valid phone number in the U.S. format *xxx-xxx-xxxx* using a regular expression pattern.

## Validate URL input

```
Sub ValidateURLInput()
    Dim userInput As Variant
```

VBA for Word 365 for practitioners. Detailed instructions how to step-by-step customize examples.

```
Dim isValidInput As Boolean
Dim urlPattern As String
Dim regex As Object

' Define the regular expression pattern for URL validation
urlPattern = "^(https?://)?(www\.)?[a-zA-Z0-9-]+\.[a-zA-Z]{2,}(/\S*)?$"

' Create a Regular Expression object
Set regex = CreateObject("VBScript.RegExp")
regex.Global = False
regex.IgnoreCase = True
regex.Pattern = urlPattern

' Prompt the user for input
Do
    userInput = InputBox("Enter a URL:")

    ' Check if the user canceled the input
    If userInput = "" Then
        MsgBox "Input canceled. Exiting."
        Exit Sub
    End If

    ' Check if the input matches the URL pattern
    If regex.Test(userInput) Then
        isValidInput = True
    Else
        MsgBox "Invalid input. Please enter a valid URL."
        isValidInput = False
    End If
Loop While Not isValidInput

' Process the valid URL input
MsgBox "You entered a valid URL: " & userInput
End Sub
```

VBA for Word 365 for practitioners. Detailed instructions how to step-by-step customize examples.

This code validates that the user enters a valid URL using a regular expression pattern.

## Validate currency input

```
Sub ValidateCurrencyInput()
    Dim userInput As Variant
    Dim isValidInput As Boolean
    Dim result As Currency

    ' Prompt the user for input
    Do
        userInput = InputBox("Enter a currency amount:")

        ' Check if the user canceled the input
        If userInput = "" Then
            MsgBox "Input canceled. Exiting."
            Exit Sub
        End If

        ' Attempt to convert the input to a Currency data type
        On Error Resume Next
        result = CCur(userInput)
        On Error GoTo 0

        ' Check if the conversion was successful
        If IsNumeric(result) Then
            isValidInput = True
        Else
            MsgBox "Invalid input. Please enter a valid currency amount."
            isValidInput = False
        End If
    Loop While Not isValidInput

    ' Process the valid currency input
```

VBA for Word 365 for practitioners. Detailed instructions how to step-by-step customize examples.

```
    MsgBox "You entered a valid currency amount: " &
Format(result, "#,##0.00")
End Sub
```

This code validates that the user enters a valid currency amount and displays it in a formatted manner.

# Working with arrays

Arrays allow you to store and manipulate multiple values of the same data type. Here's an example that stores and displays an array of names:

```
Sub ArrayExample()
    Dim names(3) As String

    names(0) = "Alice"
    names(1) = "Bob"
    names(2) = "Charlie"
    names(3) = "David"

    For i = LBound(names) To UBound(names)
        MsgBox "Name " & i + 1 & ": " & names(i)
    Next i
End Sub
```

## Options and variations

Here are some examples of tasks you can perform when counting words in Word using VBA.

Certainly! Here are some options and variations for the `Sub ArrayExample()` code, which demonstrates working with arrays in VBA:

### Use a for each loop

```
Sub ArrayExampleForEach()
    Dim names(3) As String

    names(0) = "Alice"
    names(1) = "Bob"
```

VBA for Word 365 for practitioners. Detailed instructions how to step-by-step customize examples.

```
    names(2) = "Charlie"
    names(3) = "David"


    For Each name In names
        MsgBox "Name: " & name
    Next name
End Sub
```

This code uses a *For Each* loop to iterate through the elements in the `names` array and display each name in a message box.

## Resize the array dynamically

```
Sub DynamicArrayExample()
    Dim names() As String


    ReDim names(3) ' Initialize the array with 4 elements


    names(0) = "Alice"
    names(1) = "Bob"
    names(2) = "Charlie"
    names(3) = "David"


    For i = LBound(names) To UBound(names)
        MsgBox "Name " & i + 1 & ": " & names(i)
    Next i
End Sub
```

This code initializes an array without specifying its size initially and then resizes it dynamically to hold four elements.

## Use a collection instead of an array

```
Sub CollectionExample()
    Dim names As Collection
    Set names = New Collection


    names.Add "Alice"
    names.Add "Bob"
```

VBA for Word 365 for practitioners. Detailed instructions how to step-by-step customize examples.

```
names.Add "Charlie"
names.Add "David"

For Each name In names
    MsgBox "Name: " & name
Next name
End Sub
```

This code uses a *Collection* object to store and iterate through a list of names. Collections are dynamic and can grow or shrink as needed.

## Display names in reverse order

```
Sub ReverseArrayExample()
    Dim names(3) As String

    names(0) = "Alice"
    names(1) = "Bob"
    names(2) = "Charlie"
    names(3) = "David"

    For i = UBound(names) To LBound(names) Step -1
        MsgBox "Name " & UBound(names) - i + 1 & ": " & names(i)
    Next i
End Sub
```

This code displays the names in reverse order by iterating through the array in reverse.

## Add names to the array using InputBox

```
Sub AddNamesToArray()
    Dim names() As String
    Dim nameCount As Integer

    nameCount = InputBox("Enter the number of names:")
    ReDim names(nameCount - 1)

    For i = 0 To nameCount - 1
```

```
        names(i) = InputBox("Enter name " & i + 1 & ":")
    Next i


    For i = LBound(names) To UBound(names)
        MsgBox "Name " & i + 1 & ": " & names(i)
    Next i
End Sub
```

This code allows the user to specify the number of names and then uses an input box to collect the names, which are stored in the array.

## Filter names that start with a specific letter

```
Sub FilterNamesByLetter()
    Dim names(3) As String
    Dim letter As String
    Dim filteredNames() As String
    Dim count As Integer


    names(0) = "Alice"
    names(1) = "Bob"
    names(2) = "Charlie"
    names(3) = "David"


    letter = InputBox("Enter a letter to filter names:")


    For i = LBound(names) To UBound(names)
        If Left(names(i), 1) = letter Then
            ReDim Preserve filteredNames(count)
            filteredNames(count) = names(i)
            count = count + 1
        End If
    Next i


    If count = 0 Then
        MsgBox "No names start with the letter " & letter
    Else
```

VBA for Word 365 for practitioners. Detailed instructions how to step-by-step customize examples.

```
        MsgBox "Names starting with '" & letter & "': " &
Join(filteredNames, ", ")
    End If
End Sub
```

This code allows the user to filter names that start with a specific letter and displays the filtered names in a message box.

## Modify and update names

```
Sub ModifyAndDisplayNames()
    Dim names(3) As String

    names(0) = "Alice"
    names(1) = "Bob"
    names(2) = "Charlie"
    names(3) = "David"

    Dim newName As String
    Dim index As Integer

    ' Prompt the user to select an index to modify
    index = InputBox("Enter the index (1 to 4) of the name to
modify:")

    If index >= 1 And index <= 4 Then
        ' Prompt the user for a new name
        newName = InputBox("Enter the new name:")

        ' Update the name in the array
        names(index - 1) = newName

        ' Display the modified names
        Dim modifiedNames As String
        For i = LBound(names) To UBound(names)
```

VBA for Word 365 for practitioners. Detailed instructions how to step-by-step customize examples.

```
            modifiedNames = modifiedNames & "Name " & i + 1 & ": "
& names(i) & vbNewLine
        Next i


        MsgBox "Modified Names:" & vbNewLine & modifiedNames
    Else
        MsgBox "Invalid index. Please enter a valid index between
1 and 4."
    End If
End Sub
```

This code allows the user to modify a name in the array by specifying the index and then displays the updated list of names.

## Add elements to the array

```
Sub AddElementsToArray()
    Dim names() As String
    Dim newName As String

    ReDim names(3) ' Initialize the array with 4 elements

    names(0) = "Alice"
    names(1) = "Bob"
    names(2) = "Charlie"
    names(3) = "David"


    newName = InputBox("Enter a new name:")


    ' Resize the array to add a new element
    ReDim Preserve names(UBound(names) + 1)
    names(UBound(names)) = newName


    For i = LBound(names) To UBound(names)
        MsgBox "Name " & i + 1 & ": " & names(i)
    Next i
End Sub
```

VBA for Word 365 for practitioners. Detailed instructions how to step-by-step customize examples.

This code allows the user to add a new name to the array by resizing it dynamically.

## Concatenate names into a single string

```
Sub ConcatenateNames()
    Dim names(3) As String

    names(0) = "Alice"
    names(1) = "Bob"
    names(2) = "Charlie"
    names(3) = "David"

    Dim concatenatedNames As String

    For i = LBound(names) To UBound(names)
        concatenatedNames = concatenatedNames & names(i) & " "
    Next i

    MsgBox "Concatenated Names: " & Trim(concatenatedNames)
End Sub
```

This code concatenates the names in the array into a single string and then displays the concatenated names.

## Split Names into first and last name

```
Sub SplitAndDisplayNames()
    Dim fullNames(3) As String

    fullNames(0) = "Alice Johnson"
    fullNames(1) = "Bob Smith"
    fullNames(2) = "Charlie Brown"
    fullNames(3) = "David Lee"

    Dim firstName As String
    Dim lastName As String
```

VBA for Word 365 for practitioners. Detailed instructions how to step-by-step customize examples.

```
    ' Split full names into first and last names
    For i = LBound(fullNames) To UBound(fullNames)
        Dim nameParts() As String
        nameParts = Split(fullNames(i), " ")


        If UBound(nameParts) >= 0 Then
            firstName = nameParts(0)
            lastName = nameParts(UBound(nameParts))
            MsgBox "First Name: " & firstName & vbCrLf & "Last
Name: " & lastName
        End If
    Next i
End Sub
```

This code splits full names into first and last names and then displays both parts.

These options provide variations for working with arrays and collections in VBA, including dynamic resizing, reverse order iteration, and using a `Collection` object. You can choose the one that best fits your specific needs or explore further customization based on your requirements.

# Working with Objects

Objects in VBA allow you to interact with various elements of the Word application. Here's an example that accesses the document properties:

Sub DocumentProperties()

  Dim doc As Document

  Set doc = ActiveDocument


  MsgBox "Author: " & doc.BuiltInDocumentProperties("Last Author").Value

  MsgBox "Title: " & doc.BuiltInDocumentProperties("Title").Value

End Sub

VBA for Word 365 for practitioners. Detailed instructions how to step-by-step customize examples.

# Options and variations

Here are some options and variations you can consider for the VBA code.

## Display word count and character count properties

```
Sub DocumentPropertiesWordCharCount()
    Dim doc As Document
    Set doc = ActiveDocument

    MsgBox "Word Count: " & doc.BuiltInDocumentProperties("Number
of Words").Value
    MsgBox "Character Count: " &
doc.BuiltInDocumentProperties("Number of Characters").Value
End Sub
```

This code displays the word count and character count properties of the document.

Display created and last modified properties

```
Sub DocumentPropertiesCreatedModified()
    Dim doc As Document
    Set doc = ActiveDocument

    MsgBox "Created: " & doc.BuiltInDocumentProperties("Creation
Date").Value
    MsgBox "Last Modified: " & doc.BuiltInDocumentProperties("Last
Save Time").Value
End Sub
```

This code displays the created and last modified properties of the document.

## Display document keywords and comments properties

```
Sub DocumentPropertiesKeywordsComments()
    Dim doc As Document
    Set doc = ActiveDocument
```

```
    MsgBox "Keywords: " &
doc.BuiltInDocumentProperties("Keywords").Value
    MsgBox "Comments: " &
doc.BuiltInDocumentProperties("Comments").Value
End Sub
```

This code displays the keywords and comments properties of the document.

## Display company and category properties

```
Sub DocumentPropertiesCompanyCategory()
    Dim doc As Document
    Set doc = ActiveDocument

    MsgBox "Company: " &
doc.BuiltInDocumentProperties("Company").Value
    MsgBox "Category: " &
doc.BuiltInDocumentProperties("Category").Value
End Sub
```

This code displays the company and category properties of the document.

## Display document subject and manager properties

```
Sub DocumentPropertiesSubjectManager()
    Dim doc As Document
    Set doc = ActiveDocument

    MsgBox "Subject: " &
doc.BuiltInDocumentProperties("Subject").Value
    MsgBox "Manager: " &
doc.BuiltInDocumentProperties("Manager").Value
End Sub
```

This code displays the subject and manager properties of the document.

VBA for Word 365 for practitioners. Detailed instructions how to step-by-step customize examples.

# Display document revision number and status properties

```
Sub DocumentPropertiesRevisionStatus()
    Dim doc As Document
    Set doc = ActiveDocument

    MsgBox "Revision Number: " &
doc.BuiltInDocumentProperties("Revision Number").Value
    MsgBox "Status: " &
doc.BuiltInDocumentProperties("Status").Value
End Sub
```

This code displays the revision number and status properties of the document.

# Display document template and content type properties

```
Sub DocumentPropertiesTemplateContentType()
    Dim doc As Document
    Set doc = ActiveDocument

    MsgBox "Template: " &
doc.BuiltInDocumentProperties("Template").Value
    MsgBox "Content Type: " &
doc.BuiltInDocumentProperties("Content Type").Value
End Sub
```

This code displays the template and content type properties of the document.

# Display document language and manager properties

```
Sub DocumentPropertiesLanguageManager()
    Dim doc As Document
    Set doc = ActiveDocument
```

VBA for Word 365 for practitioners. Detailed instructions how to step-by-step customize examples.

```
    MsgBox "Language: " &
doc.BuiltInDocumentProperties("Language").Value
    MsgBox "Manager: " &
doc.BuiltInDocumentProperties("Manager").Value
End Sub
```

This code displays the language and manager properties of the document.

## Display custom Document properties

```
Sub CustomDocumentProperties()
    Dim doc As Document
    Set doc = ActiveDocument

    ' Replace "CustomPropertyName" with the name of your custom
property
    MsgBox "Custom Property: " &
doc.CustomDocumentProperties("CustomPropertyName").Value
End Sub
```

This code allows you to specify a custom property name and displays its value. Replace *CustomPropertyName* with the name of your custom property.

These options demonstrate different ways to access and display various document properties, including built-in properties like Author and Title, as well as custom properties. You can choose the option that best suits your needs or combine elements from multiple options to create a customized document property viewer in VBA for Word.

# Automating Mail Merge

VBA can automate the process of performing mail merges in Word. Here's an example that performs a simple mail merge:

```
Sub MailMergeExample()
    Dim wdApp As Object
    Set wdApp = CreateObject("Word.Application")

    wdApp.Documents.Add
```

VBA for Word 365 for practitioners. Detailed instructions how to step-by-step customize examples.

```
    wdApp.Selection.TypeText "Dear <<First_Name>>,"
    wdApp.Selection.TypeText vbNewLine
    wdApp.Selection.TypeText "We are pleased to inform you that
your account balance is $<<Balance>>."
    wdApp.Selection.TypeText vbNewLine
    wdApp.Selection.TypeText "Sincerely, Your Bank"


    wdApp.ActiveDocument.MailMerge.OpenDataSource _
        Name:="C:\Path\To\Your\DataSource.xlsx", _
        SQLStatement:="SELECT * FROM [Sheet1$]"


    wdApp.ActiveDocument.MailMerge.Execute
    wdApp.ActiveDocument.Close SaveChanges:=wdDoNotSaveChanges
    wdApp.Quit


    Set wdApp = Nothing
End Sub
```

# Options and variations

Here are some options and variations you can consider for the VBA code.

## Simple mail merge with fixed data

```
Sub SimpleMailMerge()
    Dim wdApp As Object
    Set wdApp = CreateObject("Word.Application")


    wdApp.Documents.Add
    wdApp.Selection.TypeText "Dear John,"
    wdApp.Selection.TypeText vbNewLine
    wdApp.Selection.TypeText "We are pleased to inform you that
your account balance is $5000."
    wdApp.Selection.TypeText vbNewLine
    wdApp.Selection.TypeText "Sincerely, Your Bank"
```

VBA for Word 365 for practitioners. Detailed instructions how to step-by-step customize examples.

```
    wdApp.ActiveDocument.MailMerge.MainDocumentType =
wdFormLetters
    wdApp.ActiveDocument.MailMerge.OpenDataSource _
        Name:="C:\Path\To\Your\DataSource.xlsx", _
        SQLStatement:="SELECT * FROM [Sheet1$]"

    wdApp.ActiveDocument.MailMerge.Execute
    wdApp.ActiveDocument.Close SaveChanges:=wdDoNotSaveChanges
    wdApp.Quit

    Set wdApp = Nothing
End Sub
```

This code performs a simple mail merge with fixed data and a predefined recipient.

## Advanced mail merge with multiple recipients

```
Sub AdvancedMailMerge()
    Dim wdApp As Object
    Set wdApp = CreateObject("Word.Application")

    wdApp.Documents.Add

    ' Create a loop to iterate through a list of recipients
    Dim recipientList As Range
    Set recipientList =
Workbooks.Open("C:\Path\To\Your\RecipientList.xlsx").Worksheets("S
heet1").Range("A2:A10")

    For Each recipient In recipientList
        wdApp.Selection.TypeText "Dear " & recipient.Value & ","
        wdApp.Selection.TypeText vbNewLine
        wdApp.Selection.TypeText "We are pleased to inform you
that your account balance is $5000."
        wdApp.Selection.TypeText vbNewLine
        wdApp.Selection.TypeText "Sincerely, Your Bank"
```

VBA for Word 365 for practitioners. Detailed instructions how to step-by-step customize examples.

```
        wdApp.ActiveDocument.MailMerge.MainDocumentType =
wdFormLetters
        wdApp.ActiveDocument.MailMerge.OpenDataSource _
            Name:="C:\Path\To\Your\DataSource.xlsx", _
            SQLStatement:="SELECT * FROM [Sheet1$] WHERE
[Recipient]='" & recipient.Value & "'"
        wdApp.ActiveDocument.MailMerge.Execute
        wdApp.ActiveDocument.SaveAs
"C:\Path\To\Your\Output\Letter_" & recipient.Value & ".docx"
        wdApp.ActiveDocument.Close SaveChanges:=wdDoNotSaveChanges
    Next recipient

    wdApp.Quit
    Set wdApp = Nothing
End Sub
```

This code performs an advanced mail merge with multiple recipients, creating individual letters for each recipient and saving them separately.

## Mail merge with user input

```
Sub MailMergeWithUserInput()
    Dim wdApp As Object
    Set wdApp = CreateObject("Word.Application")

    ' Prompt the user for input
    Dim recipientName As String
    recipientName = InputBox("Enter recipient's name:")
    Dim balance As Double
    balance = CDbl(InputBox("Enter account balance:"))

    wdApp.Documents.Add
    wdApp.Selection.TypeText "Dear " & recipientName & ","
    wdApp.Selection.TypeText vbNewLine
    wdApp.Selection.TypeText "We are pleased to inform you that
your account balance is $" & Format(balance, "0.00") & "."
    wdApp.Selection.TypeText vbNewLine
```

VBA for Word 365 for practitioners. Detailed instructions how to step-by-step customize examples.

```
    wdApp.Selection.TypeText "Sincerely, Your Bank"


    wdApp.ActiveDocument.MailMerge.MainDocumentType =
wdFormLetters
    wdApp.ActiveDocument.MailMerge.OpenDataSource _
        Name:="C:\Path\To\Your\DataSource.xlsx", _
        SQLStatement:="SELECT * FROM [Sheet1$]"


    wdApp.ActiveDocument.MailMerge.Execute
    wdApp.ActiveDocument.Close SaveChanges:=wdDoNotSaveChanges
    wdApp.Quit


    Set wdApp = Nothing
End Sub
```

This code prompts the user for recipient information before performing the mail merge.

## Mail merge with conditional content

```
Sub ConditionalMailMerge()
    Dim wdApp As Object
    Set wdApp = CreateObject("Word.Application")


    wdApp.Documents.Add


    ' Define a condition for including content
    Dim balance As Double
    balance = CDbl(InputBox("Enter account balance:"))


    wdApp.Selection.TypeText "Dear Customer,"
    wdApp.Selection.TypeText vbNewLine


    ' Check the account balance and include content conditionally
    If balance > 5000 Then
        wdApp.Selection.TypeText "Congratulations! Your account
balance is $" & Format(balance, "0.00") & "."
```

VBA for Word 365 for practitioners. Detailed instructions how to step-by-step customize examples.

```
    Else
        wdApp.Selection.TypeText "We are pleased to inform you
that your account balance is $" & Format(balance, "0.00") & "."
    End If

    wdApp.Selection.TypeText vbNewLine
    wdApp.Selection.TypeText "Sincerely, Your Bank"

    wdApp.ActiveDocument.MailMerge.MainDocumentType =
wdFormLetters
    wdApp.ActiveDocument.MailMerge.OpenDataSource _
        Name:="C:\Path\To\Your\DataSource.xlsx", _
        SQLStatement:="SELECT * FROM [Sheet1$]"

    wdApp.ActiveDocument.MailMerge.Execute
    wdApp.ActiveDocument.Close SaveChanges:=wdDoNotSaveChanges
    wdApp.Quit

    Set wdApp = Nothing
End Sub
```

This code includes conditional content in the mail merge based on the account balance.

## Mail merge with customized subject line

```
Sub CustomSubjectMailMerge()
    Dim wdApp As Object
    Set wdApp = CreateObject("Word.Application")

    wdApp.Documents.Add
    wdApp.Selection.TypeText "Subject: Account Balance Update"
    wdApp.Selection.TypeText vbNewLine
    wdApp.Selection.TypeText "Dear Customer,"
    wdApp.Selection.TypeText vbNewLine
```

VBA for Word 365 for practitioners. Detailed instructions how to step-by-step customize examples.

```
    wdApp.Selection.TypeText "We are pleased to inform you that
your account balance is $5000."
    wdApp.Selection.TypeText vbNewLine
    wdApp.Selection.TypeText "Sincerely, Your Bank"


    wdApp.ActiveDocument.MailMerge.MainDocumentType =
wdFormLetters
    wdApp.ActiveDocument.MailMerge.OpenDataSource _
        Name:="C:\Path\To\Your\DataSource.xlsx", _
        SQLStatement:="SELECT * FROM [Sheet1$]"


    wdApp.ActiveDocument.MailMerge.Execute
    wdApp.ActiveDocument.Close SaveChanges:=wdDoNotSaveChanges
    wdApp.Quit


    Set wdApp = Nothing
End Sub
```

This code adds a custom subject line to the email-like mail merge document.

## Mail merge with envelope format

```
Sub EnvelopeMailMerge()
    Dim wdApp As Object
    Set wdApp = CreateObject("Word.Application")


    wdApp.Documents.Add
    wdApp.ActiveDocument.MailMerge.MainDocumentType = wdEnvelope
    wdApp.ActiveDocument.MailMerge.OpenDataSource _
        Name:="C:\Path\To\Your\DataSource.xlsx", _
        SQLStatement:="SELECT * FROM [Sheet1$]"


    wdApp.ActiveDocument.MailMerge.Execute
    wdApp.ActiveDocument.Close SaveChanges:=wdDoNotSaveChanges
    wdApp.Quit


    Set wdApp = Nothing
```

```
End Sub
```

This code sets up a mail merge document in an envelope format.

Mail merge with different data source

```
Sub DifferentDataSourceMailMerge()
    Dim wdApp As Object
    Set wdApp = CreateObject("Word.Application")

    wdApp.Documents.Add
    wdApp.Selection.TypeText "Dear <<First_Name>>,"
    wdApp.Selection.TypeText vbNewLine
    wdApp.Selection.TypeText "We are pleased to inform you that
your account balance is $<<Balance>>."
    wdApp.Selection.TypeText vbNewLine
    wdApp.Selection.TypeText "Sincerely, Your Bank"

    ' Use a different data source
    wdApp.ActiveDocument.MailMerge.OpenDataSource _
        Name:="C:\Path\To\Your\DifferentDataSource.xlsx", _
        SQLStatement:="SELECT * FROM [Sheet1$]"

    wdApp.ActiveDocument.MailMerge.Execute
    wdApp.ActiveDocument.Close SaveChanges:=wdDoNotSaveChanges
    wdApp.Quit

    Set wdApp = Nothing
End Sub
```

This code sets up a mail merge document in an envelope format.

## Mail merge with different data source

```
Sub DifferentDataSourceMailMerge()
    Dim wdApp As Object
    Set wdApp = CreateObject("Word.Application")

    wdApp.Documents.Add
    wdApp.Selection.TypeText "Dear <<First_Name>>,"
```

VBA for Word 365 for practitioners. Detailed instructions how to step-by-step customize examples.

```
    wdApp.Selection.TypeText vbNewLine
    wdApp.Selection.TypeText "We are pleased to inform you that
your account balance is $<<Balance>>."
    wdApp.Selection.TypeText vbNewLine
    wdApp.Selection.TypeText "Sincerely, Your Bank"

    ' Use a different data source
    wdApp.ActiveDocument.MailMerge.OpenDataSource _
        Name:="C:\Path\To\Your\DifferentDataSource.xlsx", _
        SQLStatement:="SELECT * FROM [Sheet1$]"

    wdApp.ActiveDocument.MailMerge.Execute
    wdApp.ActiveDocument.Close SaveChanges:=wdDoNotSaveChanges
    wdApp.Quit

    Set wdApp = Nothing
End Sub
```

This code performs a mail merge with a different data source.

## Mail merge with custom data mapping

```
Sub CustomDataMappingMailMerge()
    Dim wdApp As Object
    Set wdApp = CreateObject("Word.Application")

    wdApp.Documents.Add
    wdApp.Selection.TypeText "Dear <<Recipient_Name>>,"
    wdApp.Selection.TypeText vbNewLine
    wdApp.Selection.TypeText "We are pleased to inform you that
your account balance is $<<Account_Balance>>."
    wdApp.Selection.TypeText vbNewLine
    wdApp.Selection.TypeText "Sincerely, Your Bank"

    ' Define custom data mapping for placeholders
    wdApp.ActiveDocument.MailMerge.Fields.Add _
        Range:=wdApp.ActiveDocument.Content, _
```

VBA for Word 365 for practitioners. Detailed instructions how to step-by-step customize examples.

```
        Type:=wdFieldMergeField, _
        Text:="""Recipient_Name"""
    wdApp.ActiveDocument.MailMerge.Fields.Add _
        Range:=wdApp.ActiveDocument.Content, _
        Type:=wdFieldMergeField, _
        Text:="""Account_Balance"""


    wdApp.ActiveDocument.MailMerge.MainDocumentType =
wdFormLetters
    wdApp.ActiveDocument.MailMerge.OpenDataSource _
        Name:="C:\Path\To\Your\DataSourceWithCustomMapping.xlsx",
_

        SQLStatement:="SELECT * FROM [Sheet1$]"


    wdApp.ActiveDocument.MailMerge.Execute
    wdApp.ActiveDocument.Close SaveChanges:=wdDoNotSaveChanges
    wdApp.Quit


    Set wdApp = Nothing
End Sub
```

This code uses custom data mapping for placeholders in the mail merge.

## Mail merge with additional fields

```
Sub AdditionalFieldsMailMerge()
    Dim wdApp As Object
    Set wdApp = CreateObject("Word.Application")


    wdApp.Documents.Add
    wdApp.Selection.TypeText "Dear <<First_Name>>,"
    wdApp.Selection.TypeText vbNewLine
    wdApp.Selection.TypeText "We are pleased to inform you that
your account balance is $<<Balance>>."
    wdApp.Selection.TypeText vbNewLine
    wdApp.Selection.TypeText "Your Account Number is:
<<Account_Number>>."
```

VBA for Word 365 for practitioners. Detailed instructions how to step-by-step customize examples.

```
    wdApp.Selection.TypeText vbNewLine
    wdApp.Selection.TypeText "Sincerely, Your Bank"

    ' Include additional fields
    wdApp.ActiveDocument.MailMerge.Fields.Add _
        Range:=wdApp.ActiveDocument.Content, _
        Type:=wdFieldMergeField, _
        Text:="""Account_Number"""

    wdApp.ActiveDocument.MailMerge.MainDocumentType =
wdFormLetters
    wdApp.ActiveDocument.MailMerge.OpenDataSource _

Name:="C:\Path\To\Your\DataSourceWithAdditionalFields.xlsx", _
        SQLStatement:="SELECT * FROM [Sheet1$]"

    wdApp.ActiveDocument.MailMerge.Execute
    wdApp.ActiveDocument.Close SaveChanges:=wdDoNotSaveChanges
    wdApp.Quit

    Set wdApp = Nothing
End Sub
```

This code includes additional fields in the mail merge document.

## Mail merge with formatting

```
Sub MailMergeWithFormatting()
    Dim wdApp As Object
    Set wdApp = CreateObject("Word.Application")

    wdApp.Documents.Add

    ' Apply formatting to the mail merge document
    With wdApp.Selection
        .Font.Name = "Arial"
        .Font.Size = 12
```

VBA for Word 365 for practitioners. Detailed instructions how to step-by-step customize examples.

```
        .ParagraphFormat.Alignment = wdAlignParagraphLeft
    End With


    wdApp.Selection.TypeText "Dear <<First_Name>>,"
    wdApp.Selection.TypeText vbNewLine
    wdApp.Selection.TypeText "We are pleased to inform you that
your account balance is $<<Balance>>."
    wdApp.Selection.TypeText vbNewLine
    wdApp.Selection.TypeText "Sincerely, Your Bank"


    wdApp.ActiveDocument.MailMerge.MainDocumentType =
wdFormLetters
    wdApp.ActiveDocument.MailMerge.OpenDataSource _
        Name:="C:\Path\To\Your\DataSource.xlsx", _
        SQLStatement:="SELECT * FROM [Sheet1$]"


    wdApp.ActiveDocument.MailMerge.Execute
    wdApp.ActiveDocument.SaveAs
"C:\Path\To\Your\Output\MailMergeWithFormatting.docx"
    wdApp.ActiveDocument.Close SaveChanges:=wdDoNotSaveChanges
    wdApp.Quit


    Set wdApp = Nothing
End Sub
```

This code applies formatting to the mail merge document before performing the merge.

These options provide different scenarios and customizations for performing mail merge operations in VBA, including conditional content, user input, formatting, and custom data mapping. You can choose the option that best suits your specific mail merge requirements.

# Error handling

Advanced error handling techniques can help you handle errors gracefully. Here's an example that uses *On Error GoTo* to handle different types of errors:

```
Sub AdvancedErrorHandling()
```

VBA for Word 365 for practitioners. Detailed instructions how to step-by-step customize examples.

```
On Error GoTo ErrorHandler


' Code that may cause an error
Dim result As Double
result = 10 / 0 ' This will cause a runtime error


' More code
```

```
Exit Sub
ErrorHandler:
    MsgBox "An error occurred: " & Err.Description, vbExclamation,
"Error"
    Err.Clear
End Sub
```

# Options and variations

Here are some options and variations you can consider for the VBA code.

## Basic error handling

```
Sub BasicErrorHandling()
    On Error Resume Next
    ' Code that might cause an error
    Dim result As Double
    result = 1 / 0 ' Division by zero error
    If Err.Number <> 0 Then
        MsgBox "An error occurred: " & Err.Description
        Err.Clear
    End If
    On Error GoTo 0
End Sub
```

In this example, we use *On Error Resume Next* to continue execution after an error occurs, check if an error occurred with *Err.Number*, and display an error message.

# Error handling with multiple error handlers

```
Sub MultipleErrorHandlers()
    On Error GoTo ErrorHandler1
    Dim result As Double
    result = 1 / 0 ' Division by zero error
    ' Other code here
    Exit Sub ' Prevents execution of the error handler

ErrorHandler1:
    MsgBox "Error Handler 1: " & Err.Description
    Err.Clear
    On Error GoTo ErrorHandler2 ' Jump to another error handler

ErrorHandler2:
    MsgBox "Error Handler 2: " & Err.Description
    Err.Clear
    Resume Next ' Resume execution after handling the error
End Sub
```

In this example, we demonstrate how to use multiple error handlers.

# Error handling with specific error numbers

```
Sub SpecificErrorHandling()
    On Error Resume Next
    Dim result As Double
    result = 1 / 0 ' Division by zero error
    If Err.Number = 11 Then ' Division by zero error number
        MsgBox "A division by zero error occurred."
    ElseIf Err.Number = 13 Then ' Type mismatch error number
        MsgBox "A type mismatch error occurred."
    Else
        MsgBox "An unexpected error occurred: " & Err.Description
    End If
    Err.Clear
    On Error GoTo 0
```

```
End Sub
```

In this example, we handle specific error numbers differently.

## Raising custom errors

```
Sub RaiseCustomError()
    On Error Resume Next
    Dim age As Integer
    age = InputBox("Enter your age:")

    If age < 18 Then
        ' Raise a custom error
        Err.Raise vbObjectError + 9999, , "You must be 18 or
older."
    End If

    If Err.Number <> 0 Then
        MsgBox "An error occurred: " & Err.Description
        Err.Clear
    Else
        MsgBox "No error occurred."
    End If
    On Error GoTo 0
End Sub
```

In this example, we raise a custom error using *Err.Raise* when a condition is met.

## Logging errors to a file

```
Sub LogErrorsToFile()
    On Error Resume Next
    ' Code that might cause an error
    Dim result As Double
    result = 1 / 0 ' Division by zero error

    If Err.Number <> 0 Then
        Dim errorLog As Object
```

VBA for Word 365 for practitioners. Detailed instructions how to step-by-step customize examples.

```
        Set errorLog =
CreateObject("Scripting.FileSystemObject").OpenTextFile("ErrorLog.
txt", 8, True)
        errorLog.WriteLine "Error Number: " & Err.Number
        errorLog.WriteLine "Error Description: " & Err.Description
        errorLog.Close
        MsgBox "An error occurred. Details have been logged to
ErrorLog.txt."
        Err.Clear
    End If
    On Error GoTo 0
End Sub
```

This code logs errors to a text file for later analysis.

## Displaying a user-friendly error message

```
Sub UserFriendlyErrorMessage()
    On Error Resume Next
    ' Code that might cause an error
    Dim result As Double
    result = 1 / 0 ' Division by zero error

    If Err.Number <> 0 Then
        MsgBox "Oops! Something went wrong. Please contact
support." & vbCrLf & _
                "Error Number: " & Err.Number & vbCrLf & _
                "Error Description: " & Err.Description
        Err.Clear
    End If
    On Error GoTo 0
End Sub
```

This code displays a user-friendly error message.

## Error handling in a class module

```
Class ErrorHandler
    Public Sub HandleError()
```

VBA for Word 365 for practitioners. Detailed instructions how to step-by-step customize examples.

```
    On Error Resume Next
    ' Code that might cause an error
    Dim result As Double
    result = 1 / 0 ' Division by zero error

    If Err.Number <> 0 Then
        MsgBox "An error occurred: " & Err.Description
        Err.Clear
    End If
    On Error GoTo 0
End Sub
End Class
```

This example demonstrates error handling in a class module.

## Resuming execution after error

```
Sub ResumeExecutionAfterError()
    On Error Resume Next
    Dim result As Double
    result = 1 / 0 ' Division by zero error

    If Err.Number <> 0 Then
        MsgBox "An error occurred: " & Err.Description
        Err.Clear
        ' Resume execution at a specific line
        Resume NextLine
    End If
    On Error GoTo 0

NextLine:
    MsgBox "Resuming execution after error."
    ' Continue with code
End Sub
```

This code demonstrates how to resume execution after an error at a specific line.

## Centralized error handling in modules

```
Sub CentralizedErrorHandling()
    On Error Resume Next
    ' Code that might cause an error
    Dim result As Double
    result = 1 / 0 ' Division by zero error

    If Err.Number <> 0 Then
        ErrorHandler.HandleError
        Err.Clear
    End If
    On Error GoTo 0
End Sub


' Centralized error handling in a separate module
Sub HandleError()
    MsgBox "An error occurred: " & Err.Description
    Err.Clear
End Sub
```

This example demonstrates centralized error handling in a separate module.

## Graceful exit and cleanup

```
Sub GracefulExitAndCleanup()
    On Error Resume Next
    Dim fileNumber As Integer
    fileNumber = FreeFile

    Open "NonExistentFile.txt" For Input As fileNumber

    If Err.Number <> 0 Then
        MsgBox "An error occurred: " & Err.Description
        Err.Clear
        Close fileNumber ' Close the file if it was opened
    Else
```

VBA for Word 365 for practitioners. Detailed instructions how to step-by-step customize examples.

```
        ' Process the file
        Close fileNumber
    End If
    On Error GoTo 0
End Sub
```

This code gracefully exits and cleans up resources, such as file handling.

## Handling unexpected errors

```
Sub HandleUnexpectedErrors()
    On Error Resume Next
    ' Code that might cause an error
    Dim result As Double
    result = 1 / 0 ' Division by zero error

    If Err.Number <> 0 Then
        ' Handle unexpected errors by logging and displaying them
        LogError "Unexpected error occurred: " & Err.Description
        MsgBox "An unexpected error occurred. Please contact
support."
        Err.Clear
    End If
    On Error GoTo 0
End Sub


Sub LogError(errorMessage As String)
    Dim errorLog As Object
    Set errorLog =
CreateObject("Scripting.FileSystemObject").OpenTextFile("ErrorLog.
txt", 8, True)
    errorLog.WriteLine Now & ": " & errorMessage
    errorLog.Close
End Sub
```

This code handles unexpected errors by logging and displaying them, providing a better user experience.

VBA for Word 365 for practitioners. Detailed instructions how to step-by-step customize examples.

These error handling examples demonstrate various techniques and strategies for handling errors in VBA, including logging, customization and centralized error handling. Depending on your specific needs, you can adapt and combine these techniques to create robust error handling in your VBA projects.

# Working with multiple documents

You can manipulate multiple Word documents simultaneously. Here's an example that copies content from one document and pastes it into another:

```
Sub CopyContentBetweenDocuments()
    Dim sourceDoc As Document
    Dim targetDoc As Document

    ' Open or set references to source and target documents

    ' Copy content from the source document
    sourceDoc.Content.Copy

    ' Paste content into the target document
    targetDoc.Content.Paste
End Sub
```

## Options and variations

Here are some options and variations you can consider for the VBA code.

### Open a document

```
Sub OpenDocument()
    Documents.Open "C:\Path\To\Document1.docx"
End Sub
```

This code opens a specific Word document.

### Close the active document

```
Sub CloseActiveDocument()
    ActiveDocument.Close
End Sub
```

VBA for Word 365 for practitioners. Detailed instructions how to step-by-step customize examples.

This code closes the currently active Word document.

## Save changes to the active document

```
Sub SaveActiveDocument()
    ActiveDocument.Save
End Sub
```
This code saves changes to the currently active Word document.
Copy content between documents
```
Sub CopyContentBetweenDocuments()
    Dim doc1 As Document
    Dim doc2 As Document

    ' Open two documents
    Set doc1 = Documents.Open("C:\Path\To\Document1.docx")
    Set doc2 = Documents.Open("C:\Path\To\Document2.docx")

    ' Copy content from doc1 to doc2
    doc1.Content.Copy
    doc2.Content.Paste
    doc2.Save

    ' Close documents
    doc1.Close
    doc2.Close
End Sub
```
This code opens two documents, copies content from one to the other, and then saves and closes them.

## Merge documents

```
Sub MergeDocuments()
    Dim mainDoc As Document
    Set mainDoc = Documents.Open("C:\Path\To\MainDocument.docx")

    ' Merge multiple documents into the main document
```

VBA for Word 365 for practitioners. Detailed instructions how to step-by-step customize examples.

```
    mainDoc.MailMerge.OpenDataSource
Name:="C:\Path\To\DataSource.xlsx", SQLStatement:="SELECT * FROM
[Sheet1$]"
    mainDoc.MailMerge.Execute


    mainDoc.Save
    mainDoc.Close
End Sub
```

This code opens a main document and merges data from multiple documents into it.

## Loop through open documents

```
Sub LoopThroughOpenDocuments()
    Dim doc As Document
    For Each doc In Documents
        MsgBox "Document Name: " & doc.Name
    Next doc
End Sub
```

This code loops through all open documents and displays their names in a message box.

Compare two documents

```
Sub CompareDocuments()
    Dim doc1 As Document
    Dim doc2 As Document

    ' Open two documents to compare
    Set doc1 = Documents.Open("C:\Path\To\Document1.docx")
    Set doc2 = Documents.Open("C:\Path\To\Document2.docx")

    ' Compare documents and show the result
    doc1.CompareWith = "C:\Path\To\Document2.docx"
    doc1.CompareSideBySide
End Sub
```

This code opens two documents and compares them side by side.

VBA for Word 365 for practitioners. Detailed instructions how to step-by-step customize examples.

## Insert one document into another

```
Sub InsertDocumentIntoAnother()
    Dim doc1 As Document
    Dim doc2 As Document

    ' Open two documents
    Set doc1 = Documents.Open("C:\Path\To\Document1.docx")
    Set doc2 = Documents.Open("C:\Path\To\Document2.docx")

    ' Insert doc2 into doc1 at the end
    doc1.Content.InsertFile FileName:="C:\Path\To\Document2.docx"

    doc1.Save
    doc1.Close
    doc2.Close
End Sub
```

This code opens two documents and inserts one into the other at the end.

## Split a document into multiple documents

```
Sub SplitDocumentIntoMultiple()
    Dim mainDoc As Document
    Set mainDoc = Documents.Open("C:\Path\To\MainDocument.docx")

    ' Split the main document into multiple documents
    mainDoc.Range.Split Type:=wdSectionBreakNextPage

    ' Save the split documents
    For Each sec In mainDoc.Sections
        sec.Range.ExportAsFixedFormat
OutputFileName:="C:\Path\To\SplitDocument" & sec.Index & ".pdf",
ExportFormat:=wdExportFormatPDF
    Next sec

    mainDoc.Close
```

VBA for Word 365 for practitioners. Detailed instructions how to step-by-step customize examples.

End Sub

This code splits a main document into multiple documents at section breaks and saves them individually.

## Print multiple documents

```
Sub PrintMultipleDocuments()
    Dim doc As Document
    For Each doc In Documents
        doc.PrintOut
    Next doc
End Sub
```

This code prints all open documents.

These examples demonstrate various tasks you can perform with multiple documents in VBA, including opening, closing, copying content, merging, comparing, inserting, splitting, and printing documents. You can adapt these examples to automate specific document-related tasks in your Word automation projects.

# Creating and modifying styles

VBA allows you to create and apply custom styles to your documents. Here's an example that creates a new style and applies it to selected text:

```
Sub CreateAndApplyCustomStyle()
    Dim newStyle As Style
    Set newStyle =
ActiveDocument.Styles.Add(Name:="MyCustomStyle",
Type:=wdStyleParagraph)

    With newStyle
        .Font.Size = 14
        .Font.Bold = True
        .Font.Color = RGB(0, 0, 255)
    End With

    ' Apply the style to selected text
```

VBA for Word 365 for practitioners. Detailed instructions how to step-by-step customize examples.

```
    Selection.Style = ActiveDocument.Styles("MyCustomStyle")
End Sub
```

# Options and variations

Here are some options and variations you can consider for the VBA code.

## Change font family

```
Sub CreateAndApplyCustomStyle_FontFamily()
    Dim newStyle As Style
    Set newStyle =
ActiveDocument.Styles.Add(Name:="MyCustomStyle",
Type:=wdStyleParagraph)

    With newStyle
        .Font.Size = 14
        .Font.Bold = True
        .Font.Color = RGB(0, 0, 255)
        .Font.Name = "Arial" ' Change font family
    End With

    ' Apply the style to selected text
    Selection.Style = ActiveDocument.Styles("MyCustomStyle")
End Sub
```

This option changes the font family to Arial in the custom style.

## Change background color

```
Sub CreateAndApplyCustomStyle_BackgroundColor()
    Dim newStyle As Style
    Set newStyle =
ActiveDocument.Styles.Add(Name:="MyCustomStyle",
Type:=wdStyleParagraph)

    With newStyle
        .Font.Size = 14
```

VBA for Word 365 for practitioners. Detailed instructions how to step-by-step customize examples.

```
    .Font.Bold = True
    .Font.Color = RGB(0, 0, 255)
    .Shading.BackgroundPatternColor = RGB(255, 255, 0) '
Change background color to yellow
    End With


    ' Apply the style to selected text
    Selection.Style = ActiveDocument.Styles("MyCustomStyle")
End Sub
```

This option changes the background color of the custom style to yellow.

## Change alignment

```
Sub CreateAndApplyCustomStyle_Alignment()
    Dim newStyle As Style
    Set newStyle =
ActiveDocument.Styles.Add(Name:="MyCustomStyle",
Type:=wdStyleParagraph)


    With newStyle
        .Font.Size = 14
        .Font.Bold = True
        .Font.Color = RGB(0, 0, 255)
        .ParagraphFormat.Alignment = wdAlignParagraphRight '
Change text alignment to right
    End With


    ' Apply the style to selected text
    Selection.Style = ActiveDocument.Styles("MyCustomStyle")
End Sub
```

This option changes the text alignment of the custom style to right-aligned.

## Modify style for other text elements

```
Sub CreateAndApplyCustomStyle_ModifyForOtherElements()
    Dim newStyle As Style
```

VBA for Word 365 for practitioners. Detailed instructions how to step-by-step customize examples.

```
    Set newStyle =
ActiveDocument.Styles.Add(Name:="MyCustomStyle",
Type:=wdStyleParagraph)

    With newStyle
        .Font.Size = 14
        .Font.Bold = True
        .Font.Color = RGB(0, 0, 255)
    End With

    ' Modify the custom style for character formatting
    With newStyle.CharacterFormat
        .Font.Italic = True
    End With

    ' Apply the style to selected text
    Selection.Style = ActiveDocument.Styles("MyCustomStyle")
End Sub
```

This option modifies the custom style for character formatting (italic) in addition to paragraph formatting.

## Create and apply a character style

```
Sub CreateAndApplyCustomCharacterStyle()
    Dim newStyle As Style
    Set newStyle =
ActiveDocument.Styles.Add(Name:="MyCustomCharacterStyle",
Type:=wdStyleCharacter)

    With newStyle
        .Font.Size = 14
        .Font.Bold = True
        .Font.Color = RGB(0, 0, 255)
    End With

    ' Apply the character style to selected text
```

VBA for Word 365 for practitioners. Detailed instructions how to step-by-step customize examples.

```
    Selection.Style =
ActiveDocument.Styles("MyCustomCharacterStyle")
End Sub
```

This option creates and applies a custom character style.

## Modify existing style

```
Sub ModifyExistingStyle()
    ' Modify an existing style
    With ActiveDocument.Styles("Heading 1")
        .Font.Size = 16
        .Font.Color = RGB(255, 0, 0)
    End With

    ' Apply the modified style to selected text
    Selection.Style = ActiveDocument.Styles("Heading 1")
End Sub
```

This option modifies an existing style (Heading 1) and applies it to selected text.

## Create and apply a linked style

```
Sub CreateAndApplyLinkedStyle()
    Dim newStyle As Style
    Set newStyle =
ActiveDocument.Styles.Add(Name:="MyLinkedStyle",
Type:=wdStyleParagraph, _
        NextParagraphStyle:=ActiveDocument.Styles("Normal"))

    With newStyle
        .Font.Size = 14
        .Font.Bold = True
        .Font.Color = RGB(0, 0, 255)
    End With

    ' Apply the linked style to selected text
    Selection.Style = ActiveDocument.Styles("MyLinkedStyle")
End Sub
```

VBA for Word 365 for practitioners. Detailed instructions how to step-by-step customize examples.

This option creates and applies a linked style with a specified next paragraph style.

## Create and apply a table style

```
Sub CreateAndApplyTableStyle()
    Dim newStyle As TableStyle
    Set newStyle =
ActiveDocument.TableStyles.Add(Name:="MyTableStyle")

    With newStyle
        .Font.Size = 12
        .Font.Bold = True
        .Font.Color = RGB(0, 0, 255)
    End With

    ' Apply the table style to a selected table
    ActiveDocument.Tables(1).Style =
ActiveDocument.TableStyles("MyTableStyle")
End Sub
```

This option creates and applies a custom table style.

## Apply a style to specific range

```
Sub ApplyStyleToRange()
    Dim myRange As Range
    Set myRange = ActiveDocument.Range(Start:=6, End:=15)

    ' Apply the style to a specific range
    myRange.Style = ActiveDocument.Styles("MyCustomStyle")
End Sub
```

This option applies a custom style to a specific range within the document.

## Delete a custom style

```
Sub DeleteCustomStyle()
    ' Delete a custom style
```

VBA for Word 365 for practitioners. Detailed instructions how to step-by-step customize examples.

```
    ActiveDocument.Styles("MyCustomStyle").Delete
End Sub
```

This option deletes a custom style named *MyCustomStyle* from the document.

These options demonstrate different ways to create, modify, and apply custom styles in Word VBA, including character styles, linked styles, table styles, and more. You can adapt these examples to suit your specific formatting needs in Word documents.

VBA for Word 365 for practitioners. Detailed instructions how to step-by-step customize examples.

# Index

Want to know how to use a word? Want to find out what a word means? Check the website and read the appropriate chapter of this book.

VBA for Word 365 for practitioners. Detailed instructions how to step-by-step customize examples.

www.ingramcontent.com/pod-product-compliance
Lightning Source LLC
LaVergne TN
LVHW022126060326
832903LV00063B/4257